KUBLAI KHAN
CHINA'S MONGOL EMPEROR

Ancient History Textbook
Children's Ancient History

D1091759

BABY PROFESSOR
EDUCATION KIDS

Speedy Publishing LLC

40 E. Main St. #1156

Newark, DE 19711

www.speedypublishing.com

Copyright 2017

Over hundreds of years Mongol armies threatened to conquer China. One time they succeeded, under Kublai Khan. Learn more about this great leader, and what he was able to achieve.

THE MONGOL WORLD

The Mongol culture developed in the flat grasslands, or steppes, of Central Asia. Mongols were herders and expert horsemen. They were very aggressive and were quick to move against anyone who opposed them.

MONGOLIAN EAGLE HUNTERS

GENGHIS KHAN

The Mongols were a patchwork of clans, some allies and some enemies of each other, until 1206. Then the man we know as Genghis Khan managed to bring the clans together into a single force. In twenty years, the Mongols under Genghis Khan expanded their control as far west as the Caspian Sea and to the Pacific Ocean in the east. The Mongols controlled parts of northern China.

Under Genghis Khan the Mongols absorbed and adopted techniques of warfare and communications that their enemies had used. He was a great administrator, and, when he died in 1227, left an empire that functioned well despite the huge distances and many peoples and cultures it contained.

OLD CAPITAL OF GENGHIS KHAN EMPIRE

KUBLAI KHAN

EARLY YEARS

A grandson of Genghis Khan, Kublai, was born in 1215 in Mongolia. Kublai learned the traditional arts of life on horseback and mounted warfare when he was a child. He also learned philosophy and culture from tutors and others from the parts of northern China that the Mongols controlled. He developed an admiration for Chinese society and traditions, and was open to incorporating them into his own life.

RISE TO POWER

Möngke, Kublai's older brother, became Khan in 1251. Under Möngke, the Mongols conquered Iran and part of Iraq, and expanded their holdings in southeast Asia. Möngke was the last khan to try to control the empire from its old capital of Karakorum in Mongolia.

Möngke put Kublai in charge of the northern part of China that the Mongols already controlled, and there Kublai gathered Chinese advisers and studied Chinese culture. He was a different sort of Mongol ruler, treating conquered peoples with much more interest and respect than had been the Mongol custom.

Kublai led the Mongol armies against the main part of China, fighting hard to add the Song dynasty's territories to the Mongol Empire. In 1259, while at war, he learned that Möngke had died. He also learned that their younger brother, Ariq Böke, was in Karakorum trying to get himself declared the Great Khan.

SONG DYNASTY TOWN

Kublai quickly made a treaty with the Song Chinese to end the fighting, and went to Karakorum himself. There he outmaneuvered his younger brother. He was declared Great Khan in 1260. However, a civil war broke out between Kublai's supporters and those supporting his brother, and Kublai did not defeat Ariq Böke until 1264. He spared his brother's life, but had all of Ariq Böke's main supporters put to death.

THE WISE KHAN

Now secure as leader of the Mongol Empire, Kublai moved the capital from Karakorum to Dadu, which is now Beijing, the capital of China. He adopted the government structures the Chinese people were used to, with levels and layers of administrators appointed mostly by merit rather than based on family connections.

THE CENTER CITY IN BEIJING CHINA

SILK ROAD

His rule showed respect for religious diversity and emphasized an expansion of trade with Europe using the Silk Road. Read more about this in the Baby Professor book Trade and Commerce in Ancient China: the Grand Canal and the Silk Road.

During this time the government greatly improved roads and water systems, and expanded the use of paper money. Kublai proclaimed a social structure of four classes. At the top were Mongol aristocrats and their families, who did not have to pay taxes. At the bottom were average Chinese laborers, who had to do most of the manual labor and who paid heavy tax rates.

CONQUESTS AND FAILURES

Kublai wanted to complete the project of uniting China under Mongol leadership. In 1267 he reopened the war with South China's Song Dynasty.

It was a long and expensive war. Mongol cavalry were not well-suited to the terrain of south China. The Song strongholds were well-defended, so the Mongols had to develop better catapults and siege weapons to batter down the walls and crush the defending troops. Some places could only be reached by crossing broad rivers or by sea, and the Mongols had a small navy at the start of the struggle.

MONGOLIAN ARCHER

However, the Mongols rose to the occasion, adopting or adapting weapons and tactics to suit where they had to fight, and expanding their navy greatly. By 1279 they had defeated the Song Dynasty. Now the Mongols ruled a united China, as well as all their other possessions.

Kublai Khan marked the victory by proclaiming a new Chinese dynasty, the Yuan, with himself as the first emperor. This dynasty lasted less than one hundred years, a very short time in Chinese terms.

Things went far less well with two other efforts. Kublai wanted to take control of Japan, and of the huge Indonesian island of Java, and the results were the Mongols' worst failures.

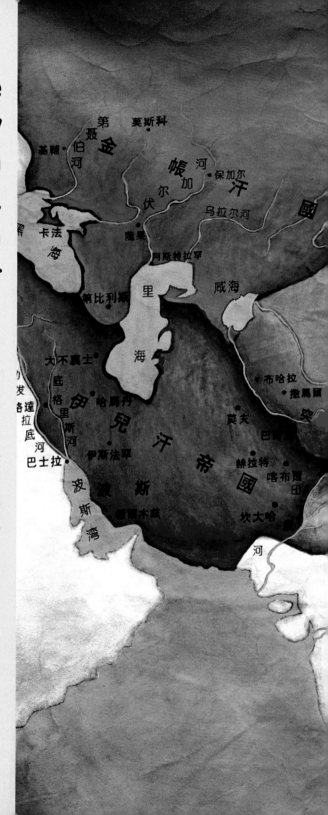

ANCIENT MAP OF CHINESE YUAN DYNASTY

MAP OF JAPAN

JAPAN

The Mongols invited Japan to agree that the Yuan Emperor was overlord of Japan, and Japan quite reasonably rejected the idea. So Kublai sent fleets of ships twice to try to conquer Japan.

In 1281 a huge Mongol fleet carrying more than 140,000 troops set out from ports in north and south China. The whole fleet gathered near Kyushu Island and it seemed unstoppable. But a typhoon (the Japanese name for a huge Pacific storm, that also means "wind from God") passed through the area, sinking many of the ships and wrecking others. More than half of the troops drowned or were captured on the coasts of Japan. The rest made it back to China.

KYUSHU ISLAND, JAPAN

JAVA, INDONESIA

JAVA

In 1292 Kublai sent a huge fleet to conquer Java, and the troops landed and made some progress. But after less than a year, the Chinese gave up. The land was far hotter and more humid than they were used to, and they were not prepared for the biting insects, the jungles, and the infections that killed off thousands of soldiers. This was not at all like fighting in the plains of central Russia!

THE END OF AMBITION

Many Chinese and some Mongolians appreciated the way Kublai Khan ran the empire, but others resented him. Many Mongols felt he had abandoned the ways of his people and had become a tool of foreigners.

Kaidu, a cousin, had a claim to the throne. He felt he was a more valid Mongol than this kimono-wearing, tea-drinking emperor. He never managed to overthrow Kublai Khan, or even come close, but he was a constant threat.

The poorer people in China deeply resented the heavy taxes they had to pay, especially when the money went to huge and expensive failures like the invasions of Japan and Java.

As Kublai got older, the weight of failure combined with personal losses like the death of his oldest son and his favorite wife, who died in 1281, and his oldest son, who died in 1288. He became gloomy, and began to drink and eat far too much. As a result he became overweight and his health began to fail.

In 1294, not long after the Mongols withdrew from their failed invasion of Java, Kublai Khan died. He was 79. He had inherited a huge empire, and made it even larger while improving the way it ran.

THE EARTH CASTLE BUILT IN YUAN DYNASTY

OLD MONK TEACHING YOUNG MONKS

KUBLAI KHAN FACTS

- Kublai Khan's fascination with China went back to his youth. He invited scholars and writers from China to visit and talk with him in Mongolia. In 1242, a monk spent a long time teaching him Buddhist philosophy.

- Another scholar, Liu Bingzhong, taught Kublai Taoist religious principles and lessons about painting, poetry, and mathematics.
- When Kublai Khan became depressed and started to withdraw from direct governing of the empire, he named his son Zhenjin as the next emperor. But Zhenjin died eight years before his father did. This deepened Kublai's sorrow.

A GIRL PRAYING IN CHURCH.

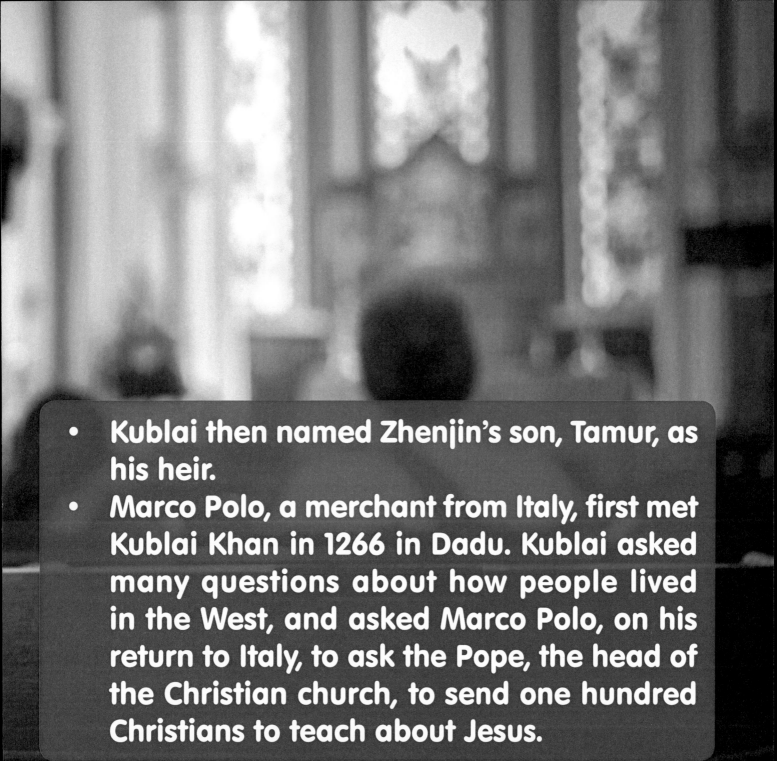

- **Kublai then named Zhenjin's son, Tamur, as his heir.**
- **Marco Polo, a merchant from Italy, first met Kublai Khan in 1266 in Dadu. Kublai asked many questions about how people lived in the West, and asked Marco Polo, on his return to Italy, to ask the Pope, the head of the Christian church, to send one hundred Christians to teach about Jesus.**

- From 1271 until about 1292, Marco Polo and his brother served as special envoys for Kublai Khan, traveling widely for him and bringing back reports on lands and peoples. When Marco Polo finally returned to Europe in 1294, he wrote an account of his travels and discoveries. This introduced Kublai Khan and the Chinese-Mongolian world to Europeans for the first time.

MARCO POLO

BOY WITH A REINDEER IN NORTHERN MONGOLIA

THE IMPACT OF KUBLAI KHAN

Kublai Khan both expanded Mongol territory and changed the Mongol world view. He helped the Mongol people move from a nomadic life to a settled life among cities and farmland. He combined the fierce Mongol spirit with the philosophies and traditions of Chinese culture.

Read more about the Chinese culture that the Mongols encountered and absorbed in Baby Professor books like How Did Your Chinese Ancestors Live? and The Chinese Festivals.

Visit

BABY PROFESSOR
EDUCATION KIDS

www.BabyProfessorBooks.com

to download Free Baby Professor eBooks
and view our catalog of new and exciting
Children's Books

Made in the USA
Middletown, DE
22 February 2018